# *As Long As We're Here*

❖

William Greenway

*FUTURECYCLE PRESS*
*www.futurecycle.org*

*Cover photo by Donald Tong; cover and interior design by Diane Kistner; PT Serif text and Courgette titling*

Library of Congress Control Number: 2022938124



Published by FutureCycle Press
Athens, Georgia, USA

ISBN 978-1-952593-32-1

*for Rosie and Mommy*

## Contents

### 1. Coca-Cola Redbone

Accidents....9
High Heaven....10
Forepray....12
The Christening....13
The Encumbrance of Things Past....14
One Hundred Years of Gratitude....16
All Through the Night....17
My Own Mary....18
A Little Welsh....19
Snug Harbor....20
A Few Thoughts on Death....22
In the Library....24
Fossils....25

### 2. Dreaming the Dead

Intrusions....29
The Welcoming....30
Overtime....31
Dreaming the Dead....32
The Unusual Dreams....34
Home Is the Sailor, Home from the Sea: Two Elegies....35
Casualty....38
Hugs....39

### 3. Diminishing Returns

The Bone-House....43
Diminishing Returns....44
Quarantines....46
Coma....49
Murmurs....50
Migraine....51
Near Florence....52
The Gospel of Judas....54

The Ghost of Christmas Past....55
Tats....56
The Late Watch....57

## *4. A World with a Mind of Its Own*

Blind Pass....61
Deep....62
Shark Week....63
St. Simons....64
Running on Water....65
A World with a Mind of Its Own....66
Blind River....68
Yeti....70
Aeolus....71
Going Amish....72
Pastorals....74
Advent in Ephrata....76

## *5. Everything We Bring, All We Leave Behind*

As Long As We're Here....81
Everything We Bring, All We Leave Behind....82
Back Then....84
Spooky Nook Road....85
Sticks....86
The 18th Hole....88
That Night at Barnacle Bill's....89
The Ghosts of Christmas Passed....90

# 1.

# Coca-Cola Redbone

## *Accidents*

She wasn't supposed to happen—
poor-white mother, the black father
split (hit it and quit it),
Opelika, Alabama.
Almost in time for that other birth
(alleged) in this snowy season,
though cotton-bearded shepherds
in bedsheets, bespectacled Magi,
and plywood mangers abound.
The Assisted Living crèche
has real sheep, goats, a mangy
camel, even a homesick llama
bowing to the rubber baby.

An angel announced the news—
unto us a social worker,
underpaid angel of a kind.
And then the long ride
back home to Bethlehem,
Pennsylvania. Okay,
to Youngstown, Ohio,
no star to guide us, but
a GPS to bounce one off of.

However these little deities arrive,
they change everything—
mostly lives—
and no matter how much
we don't want this comfy old world
to pass away,
it always does,
and the new one will always
take us with it.

# *High Heaven*

*He who loves gives a hostage to fortune.*
*—Nietzsche*

Another stinking diaper to thank
God for, why we trekked all the way to Opelika,
Alabama, to get this,
slept in a crummy motel for a month waiting
for her to be born, mud-wrestled every bureaucrat
in the state, pressing inky fingers on every piece
of paper they sent to Montgomery, endured stares
and questions: "Is she colored?" the white maid asks—
a word I haven't heard since my Georgia
cracker youth. Then another:
"But she's a pretty little pickaninny.
And don't ever cut her hair—
it'll just make it kinky."

We named her after Rosa Parks and Harper Lee.
The old black man in the doctor's office says,
"She gonna be a Coca-Cola redbone,"
a term we've never heard.
"You better keep them boys away."

Now she's crawling into every trouble there is,
and I remember why I've waited this long
for what I always feared:
loving something so much
you could die from it, this joy
at the last, at sixty-six.

I always wondered what would "curdle the blood,"
but midway through the baby poem I swore
I'd never write, and halfway down

the hall, she's trying to unplug the smoke
detector and shrieking to high heaven—not
in pain, but simply because she's found
her new voice, her own language,
and is already on her way, away.

## *Forepray*

*"Compared to a child with cancer, all your problems are just gnats on your ass."*
*—Conrad Dobler, former New Orleans Saint*

It's too late to pray for the things I want,
so I'm left to pray only
for the things I don't want:
death, disease, divorce, destitution,
all the big D's.
There'll be no more travel,
new car, job, home,
or, in so many words—one,
in fact—no more money.

Or the things money *can't* buy:
a love affair, a Nobel Prize,
or some other third thing
I haven't even imagined yet,
though when I do
I will be sadder still.

Still, I watch the evening news to see
people worse off, buried in earthquakes,
drowned in floods,
and so I pray anyway, if only
to be granted gratitude for
a lifetime of preschool fees,
mortgage, marriage, humdrum job, all
I hear humming around me
like a tiny choir.

## *The Christening*

I was just a tot when the two preachers—
my Baptist daddy and *his* daddy, Welsh
Methodist—wrangled over how much water
it takes to get us into heaven.
So at seven ("The Age
of Accountability"), I walked the aisle
"Just As I Am"
then thumbed my nose
in prayer as preacher Daniel dunked me
in the Jordan River painted
poorly on the white-washed wall
behind the choir loft,
my grandfather (or father) by then
either singing in glory or spitted
and singeing above the flames.

Now, finally parents ourselves,
we worry about the babe, our only one—
how we'd hate to see her in hell
with us—but her little bath comes only
halfway up, a wail the only tongue she speaks
when, our hearts stopping,
her head yet again
hits the hardwood.

So, with no priest or preacher
to say *yea* or *nay,*
looks like we have the job ourselves,
either in the soapy bubbles
of the bathtub Jordan
or with the sloshed gin of Happy Hour,
to prepare this trinity
for whatever heaven
or hardwood
awaits us all.

## *The Encumbrance of Things Past*

All the unhappy memories make me sad,
as do the happy ones.
When my head hits the pillow,
the cancan queue streaming between my ears
becomes a conga line of accusations,
like drunken conventioneers convened every night
wearing the white shoes, belts, and bell-bottoms
of a distant, dismal past.

After the car accident that tipped
my mother over into the dementia
that would kill her, the attic of her brain,
full of the stuff of what was,
was locked up.
Memories lived now only in that house—
*not this house, but my happy house*
*over there*—only there was no *over there*
over there, never had been.

Grandmama had one of the first
lobotomies, became quite chipper at the end,
but could never remember her husband
of forty years.

These same genes are probably circling
in the helix, the spiral staircase climbing
into my own gray garret, so that
when my daughter gets pissed at me
once again, attacking my books
on the bedside table and
stomping on my *Swann's Way,*
maybe someday she'll come to know

that Proust never wanted to go to bed
either, and that connection will be the neuron,
axion, whatever, as if she has eaten something,
a cookie maybe, whose taste takes her back
to the now, to the love her father had for her
once upon a time.

## *One Hundred Years of Gratitude*

As she watches through the window,
Pappy, Huckleberry Hound hat on,
shovels snow off the back deck,
and I wonder if this memory, of all
the others, will be her first—like Daddy
walking down the hill from the rental cabin
to take me home or my towering grandfather
clucking in the pearled pink snail
of his teeth, looking down and saying
"You Dutchman, you,"
though he was Irish.

Not some special time, I hope—
not a stuffing Christmas day nor candle-
snuffing third birthday—though
there are kids, I guess,
who live in a money-feathered nest
of Magic Kingdoms, Disney days
and firework princess nights,
the jingle-belled hooves and snowy thump
of Santa's boots on the roof every night,
every day three-rings of enchantment until,
inevitably, the circus leaves town.

I hope for her, instead, some
banal but beautiful image—
okay, maybe snowy, but also
Huckleberry Hounded—just another
life, usual, boring, ordinary, but momentarily
magic, magically
momentary.

## *All Through the Night*

No atheists in foxholes
nor near the flames of infant fevers.
*Guardian angels around my bed*
sang Mario Lanza (written by Harpo Marx!)
on an old black, shellac 78.

Only a fool would still believe
in those old wives' tales, but,
growing up in a Holy Ghost-haunted house,
how to outgrow them? No more
kneeling by the bedside, no Brahms lullaby,
no Welsh grandfather singing *sleep my child*
*and peace attend thee, all through the night.*

But how I miss those lilies
of the field, hairs numbered,
sparrows falling.

Now, my daughter sleeping in the next room,
I'd give the rest of my life, even sell
my soul to some devil or other,
for—round her bed, wielding swords,
all of them flaming—legions
of the angels I don't believe in.

## *My Own Mary*

My daughter, with her huge Afro,
is a weird Madonna in the kindergarten
Christmas pageant this year.
Since she always says she wants to marry me,
I guess that makes me Joseph—
though I feel we don't really belong here
amid all these young millennials,
me old as Methuselah, her,
half-breed (no room in this inn)—
but after "Away in a Manger,"
as the other kids file off the stage,
a little white shepherdess
bends down and kisses the swaddled,
nappy-haired dark rubber baby
my own dark Mary is holding.

# *A Little Welsh*

So far she only knows her cat
is a *moggy,* that the hated goodnight
is *Nos Da,* and though she was born half-black
and adopted poor white,
I want to give her my grandfather
who, raised in a little mountain town
where kids of all ages now
swagger around in hiking boots
and down vests, descended
every morning by cage
deep into the black earth
and walked back five miles in the dark.
Hilly Alabama
reminded him of home.

So I try to pass on, not my genes,
but my *memes*—and maybe even poems
if she ever cares to look them up.
I want the sounds of Dylan Thomas, Hopkins
to babble in her blood
as she grows.

When I tell strangers in Walmart she's Welsh,
they say "Oh, what a beautiful color,"
and the news last night had a report
from "Whales."

So if she can have a grandpa (*hen-daid*) from whales,
then he can have a grandchild (*wyres*)
from Opelika with a lilt
and skin the color of coal dust.

## *Snug Harbor*

In the photo somebody took
just after she was born,
the nurse is handing her to me
out in the hallway.
I have my arms folded across my chest,
my hands in my armpits, as if I'm cold,
or protecting my heart, or afraid to either hold,
have, or love her.
Born too early and, I thought, too late
for me, she's the size of a deflated football
and, blind as usual, I look
like I'm doubting she'll live.

A week ago, on an almost ill-fated
fishing trip, after we'd left the picturesque
little Erie harbor and passed the old lighthouse,
the weather turned bad, and I thought of "The Open Boat,"
Shackleton's ordeal, and other shipwreck disasters,
until a vision came to me through the storm,
out of the black clouds as the wave-troughs
cracked my backbone like some
incompetent chiropractor.
Oh, we caught fish, all right, but not the clear,
blue-green saltwater sort I love—
only bottom-smelling, white-cataracted walleyes.

But it wasn't my whole life that passed
before my eyes. Instead,
I wanted just one scene from an otherwise
B movie, a do-over, a retake—
to run the film back to that hallway,
to that moment, and clutch her
for the first time

knowing what I know now, and cling
to her for life in my final minutes—
so that if this trip turned fatal,
I would still sail away
but to the Western Isles instead
and steam into some safe harbor,
a tired old hulk,
the only cargo in my hold
her face.

# *A Few Thoughts on Death*

*"After the first death, there is no other."*

My daughter's new toy
is my blood-pressure cuff,
which she pumps until
she triumphantly announces,
"You're dead!"
Then I head- and tongue-loll,
though my eyes must remain closed
as if I am sleeping,
though the blue pallor and white lips
are beyond the skill of the living.

On the drive home from kindergarten
yesterday, a skunk
crossed the road in front of me—
no need to guess about
this old man's omen.

The other parents look like
they're about 16, fathers
trendy with buzz cuts and beards,
their wives chubby
with perennial pregnancy.
They think I'm the grandfather,
and I could have been if
I hadn't thought children
an anchor, instead of a lifeboat.

Nothing worse than an old timer
with new regrets.

So when she asks me what death is,
I blather on about endless sleep,
of Grandma in heaven, or
someplace of equivalent beauty

(or boredom). And when she asks
if it is going to hurt, I say no
and hope, for her at least, it's quick
and painless, just another Little Old
Ladybug on God's Great Windshield,
and pray that her next death
be like the first, that slippery slide
down, from the kinder garden of Eden,
a long dark tunnel
toward a rumor of light.

## *In the Library*

Because I got lost
in a crowded department store near Christmas,
I understand why my daughter
became so frightened today
and why I found her weeping, wandering
the stacks, looking for me,
when I was only in the restroom.

I remember searching all those faces
for my mother's, and even the shoes
coming down the escalator.
I must have thought she'd abandoned me
or died, leaving me all alone
in the world, wondering,
like my daughter, where we go—
and not a single one of all those books
has the answer.

## *Fossils*

I try to get my daughter to take
one of my books to show and tell,
a proud moment
I always dreamed of,
but she rolls her eyes
in her new sign language
and takes instead another
stuffed animal.

Or at least to take the two ammonites
we bought in Lyme Regis, the snail
shells curled and ribbed
like fetal vertebrae still here,
flesh gone.

But fossils to her are just more rocks,
and what's a million years, three
to be exact, to a young girl
with a boyfriend already—
in the 2nd grade—who, she knows,
will never be as old
as her old man.

And, after all, she's right:
a poem is really nothing.
Just another shell,
the flesh gone.

# 2.

# Dreaming the Dead

## *Intrusions*

I rolled out of bed this morning,
hitting my head on the bedside table,
which was better than being squashed
by the train. I can still feel the crossties
down my back—big ribs—my arms
outstretched across the chill rails
like the steel nails of a crucifixion.

They always seem to come from behind:
Freddy Krueger, Mother
with her garden rake, the rabid dog,
lion, rhino, zombie, sneaking up.
Either flee or fight.
*What are you afraid of,* the therapist asks,
and I answer, *ontologically, apocryphally,*
*or alphabetically?*

In Scotland, the Lairds spiraled the stone
staircases of their keeps with steps
and risers unequal to slow invaders down (or
at least to sound the clanking alarums of sword
and shield) and, at best, confound them utterly,
pile them into one another's backs
like Keystone Kops.

My therapist says, *Well, it's good*
*you're not dreaming of overflowing*
*toilets anymore.*
*No,* I say, *it's not inside,*
*but out there in the dark*
*of every night,*
waiting for their chance, for sleep,
while I listen again for steam whistles
or the stumble of steps.

## *The Welcoming*

When Matt died in a head-on some thirty years ago,
I wanted to ask my long-dead preacher father
*Why?* Another one of those questions
I used to bug him with, getting answers
that made no sense to me, about Heaven
and Eternity:
What do you do?
*Glorify God.*
For how long?
*Forever.*
How long is that?
*Forever.*

Pint-sized Inquisitor,
I persisted (permission
to badger the witness?):
Will we be ourselves, and, if so,
how old will we be?

I forgot what he said,
but it was my sister Sherry
who finally gave me the answer
I wanted, when, in hospice,
with her last breath,
she closed her eyes
and smiled
as if she'd just met *Glory*
and *Forever*
head-on
and called them what
we called him as a child:
*Matthew.*

## *Overtime*

I never got a chance to thank
those EMTs who somehow
got to that little Welsh village
so soon after the stroke, put
the tube into her throat
and, with what looked like
a clear American football, squeezed
air into her lungs, though
it was fourth down and fifty
with only seconds left.

They said at the hospital
that she was already dead,
then not, then surely by morning,
depending on which doctor came
into the fluorescent waiting room.

So I prayed to any god that was handy—
especially in the little chapel full
of Welsh Methodists, who love rugby,
the earthbound clusterfuck of the scrum,
the line-out, the maul, the try.

But we were Americans. We knew
they didn't know about the kind of bomb
you can catch, and they certainly
had never heard,
until we taught them,
about the Hail Mary
and how, sometimes, it works.

## *Dreaming the Dead*

They won't leave me alone
and come each night as if Charon
won't take them, all they owned
pawned, all their coin
already palmed by strip-mall
loan sharks.

And so they linger here
above me in the dark,
my father on the shore,
backbone still stiff
with *Nos*,
Mother a wisp, as if,
now lightened by the loss
of all her memories,
she could drift
over the dark waters.
My sister sits, shriveled
and shrouded from the crossfire
shouting of many nights,
and my brother slumps,
all money gone
first up his nose,
then into his veins.

They beckon
or bully
all night
out of loneliness,
not love,
missing even the miscreant
who meant to save them all

and failed.
They long for the happiness
they never found,
still dream of being reborn—
or at least finding
some rest—
if only they can commandeer
the boat of my bed
or my bier
to ferry them finally across.

## *The Unusual Dreams*

*Stop taking Plavix if you have unusual dreams.*

No, just the usual stuff: being
chased through burning buildings
by bolt-necked monsters,
having sex with my mother
in a sleeping bag above the eye-rolling
Confederate generals carved on the side
of Stone Mountain,
my red-headed high school sweetheart-
turned-bank clerk hitting the panic button
to have me taken away for good.

One wonders what would be unusual:
a holiday dinner without the spicing of shouts
and tears? My dead father
saying *yes* for once?
A door you don't need to squirm through
before the birth-torc tightens
around your throat
full of the words
choking to be heard?

## *Home Is the Sailor, Home from the Sea: Two Elegies*

1.

This country road I'm walking down
suddenly shimmers into the flight deck
of the now-defunct USS Ticonderoga,
Santa Catalina Island off in the blue haze,
bald California hills behind me folding
down into the cold sapphire sea,
even though it's August, which is probably why
the deck is griddle hot, and the flaming ass-ends
of blasting jets bring the tar of every seam
to a bubble.
I'm wearing those Mickey Mouse ears
amid the roar of A-4s and F-8s,
but I'm damn near deaf anyway
here at the end.

Though not especially patriotic,
I wear my "Navy Veteran" ball cap in Walmart,
hiding the gray hair, hoping to be seen as hot shit
instead of just old, maybe get a little respect
from all these young mothers and their skiving,
draft-dodging husbands, which—fair play—
I tried to be back in those interesting times.

They did a poll of the Brits' favorite paintings
a few years ago, and, surprisingly, the winner
was not one of Hopkins' "sweet especial
rural scenes," like Constable's transcendent "Hay Wain"
or "The Cornfield," you know, border collies
and sheep, those captured heavenly moments
of country peace and quiet—

nor even "Stag at Bay," a creature
hounded, trapped and doomed,
though noble to the end.

No, it was of another kind of ending, Turner's
mighty ship, "The Fighting Temeraire,"
being steamboat-towed to the scrap heap
to be dismantled bone by bone,
though Turner paints it gowned
in smoke and crowned by clouds
as if no one has told Her yet
that She'll be fighting no more.

2.

*The USS Fitzgerald*

Four young sailors trapped, drowned,
their big destroyer rammed
in darkness by a Goliath cargo ship.
Sudden darkness now inside, the door
jammed closed, frigid water first
at the ankles, then calves, then thighs,
belly, heart, lips, eyes.

That could have been me
fifty years ago.
Films in boot camp showed us
cut in half by the cables of the deck's
arresting gear, then fires
like the Forrestal's,
the crew beneath the flight deck fried.

Though my war was no closer than theirs,
no kamikaze Zeros,
mines, or torpedoes,

I still slept uneasy
in one of the “racks” stacked for space
on canvas slabs like in a morgue
while jets thumped overhead all night.

I write it here: Rigsby, Douglass,
Huynh, Hernandez, Sibayan, Martin, Rehm,
their photos on the morning news,
all jaunty in their dress blues,
from now on seen only on the mantelpiece
or in the dark of drawers,
purses, wallets, and albums
where the light will never come.

## *Casualty*

*William Henry Greenway, Reverend, 1920-1974*

The Jeep bounced him high
and, when he came down,
his back was broken. A body cast
and Red Cross cigarettes for months
and, for the rest of his life, a ruptured
diaphragm, the pain so bad,
many nights he slept sitting up.
As a boy, I saw him once
almost collapse when his nephew
gave him a bear hug.
The government did not help,
nor did his prayers.

When his heart failed, too soon,
the doctor said the bulge
had pressed on his heart like
scar tissue from a battle
or a deformity from birth,
like a club foot, or a humpback,
which heroes sometimes have.

## *Hugs*

I can't imagine, on this autumn morning,
ever waiting with my father
on cold corners for school buses,
much less hugging him
goodbye as I do my daughter.
(O lucky, lucky bus
to be able to enfold her body
into your own.)

Seems like everybody does it
these days, even jocks.
That kid there, as tall, hugs
his old man and gets hugged
back.

Only as he lay dying
did he reach
for my hand.

After the bus leaves,
I walk back home alone, along a path
already white with frost.

# 3.

# Diminishing Returns

## *The Bone-House*

It's what that olden poet
called the body, *bānhūs,* soft shell
of flesh housing the hard framework,
like the two-by-fours
I used to nail into two-stories
to get through college.
All my joints—jaw, knees, elbows, ankles—
clicking now like a room full
of typewriters, writing the saga,
I suppose, of my own ending
moldering in the grave, or
as charcoal briquets in the ashes
of the crematorium,
only what bony Beowulf
had left for the final fight
with the breath of a dragon.

## *Diminishing Returns*

*...and though*
*We are not now that strength which in old days*
*Moved earth and heaven; that which we are, we are...*
*—"Ulysses," Tennyson*

After struggling a while to follow my
7ths, 9ths, 5ths, whatever—our real
musician, the mandolin *meister,* yells,
"I feel like I'm in diminished hell!"

Wednesday will mark my sixtieth year
to heaven, the oldest of this band
of brothers. I remember learning
"500 Miles" on a guitar I had not yet
learned to tune. The same weird chords
I play now, but then, as if someone
from a previous life were playing
a dirge in Chinese:
*If you miss the train I'm on,*
*You will know that I am gone...*

When my mother told my butcher
grandfather—racist, blackjack sticking
from his back pocket—that
he was going there if he didn't
change his ways, accept Jesus as
his personal savior, he'd always say,
"But I'm already in hell."

Though it didn't sound that bad: bathtub
gin and a pickled hot pepper
in his left hand whenever he ate,
even waffles, his wife Mamie
and the wives of other men—

including the one he brained
with a ketchup bottle as he stocked
the shelves—until a stroke and blindness,
the untuned song
of his final diminishment.

## *Quarantines*

1.

Imagine the media coverage
of the Black Death, whole
families boarded up to die inside,
the comic bring-out-your-dead carts,
cameras on location by the mass graves,
Shakespeare, the Globe closed,
Lear televised to the yokels.

Tired of YouTube, my bored
daughter draws over and over
stick figures with straw hair
like the thatch of the round
red hut in a boma,
outside whose prickly perimeter
patient lions pace.

2.

The rest of us cower (cringe, grovel,
quail) inside, while out on the highway,
the hiccups (hiccoughs?) of Harleys
changing gears, flaunting
the bravado of bare faces.

3.

A far-off murmuring
has been going all morning,
like a rumor or maybe a mower
over a lawn with no end.

Or as if all our ears
are being held
to the same shell.

Or maybe now we're just
hearing it, the giant mosquito
that never bloats
on earth-blood, this buzz
of invisible things.

4.

A bad patch the British say,
like black ice on a curve, or,
the rubber band-aid
we used to patch flats,
hoping to make it
to the greasy garage on the edge
of that shabby little Western town
called Calamity
I can see from up here
on the ledge.

5.

*"My hunger, Anne, Anne, Flee on Your Donkey"*
*—Rimbaud*

The Feast of Hunger, how starving
explorers in the frozen north
and south, dreamed, not of wives
and children, but food, dreams
that dogged their tracks
until even the dogs were eaten
before they died.

Even murderers get a last meal
but on the news this morning
I learn the locusts have come back
to Egypt, stripping the land
right down to the beasts and berries,
leaving only the blood and bones,
the leftovers.

6.

She's been waiting so long
out there, wings drooping, almost
too sodden to soar anymore, white
gown grown opaque, as if
left in the sun too long,
and tinged yellow from some
old wedding.
When I see her head bowed
and blurry through the window,
blonde hair disheveled, dripping,
with so many tears to be told
in raindrops, so tired of waiting,
waiting out there, finally, for the smear
of lamb's blood on the lintel
washing away in the rain.

## *Coma*

*The hawk on fire hangs still...*
*—Dylan Thomas*

For the two months she was either down deep
or probably dead, each morning I'd wind
to the hospital through a dozen villages
to walk the halls of the I.C.U.—
or some such Welsh acronym—to sit all day
by her bedside, breaking only
for the stodge in the cafeteria, or to exit
the back way past two tall chimneys
of the crematorium
to get into the hills of South Wales,
its sheep, horses, and a few cows
black-smoke-shadowed by what
remained of the once-sick,
the grief-sick left behind.

*From the smoke into the smother,*
I heard someone quote Shakespeare
in the waiting room.

I somehow thought the country
of my preacher grandfather might enlist
his help, but being neither Church
nor Chapel, I could pray only
to the hawk that always seemed to hang
above the pastures, a windhover,
a Christless cross,
my only prayer my learning,
though I knew it never
works that way,
though maybe, for just this once,
it would, that hawk hovering high
and still above the smoke.

## *Murmurs*

Every time I come into his office—
after he shines his pencil light in my eyes,
ears, throat, nostrils—
the doc calls in the pre-meds,
who look to be about twelve years old,
and gives them the pop quiz
(me), makes them listen and listen,
with their new sphygmomanometers
chill limpets on my chest,
for the echo-y susurration, slight
stutter, hitch in heart,
like small gasps after plunges
in icy water.

Afterwards, backs to me,
they clump and mumble about
this secret they think
I don't know over in my corner alone,
as if I can't hear that backwash, lisp,
that's been whispering in me
from the very beginning.

## *Migraine*

Another one stalking her,
bringing its auras
like halos from hell.

My forebears only gave me
grandma's "sugar," Mama's thyroid,
some uncle's tremors, hallucinations,
tinnitus, the scourges of all
those old dead doctors,
Menière, Eckbom, Parkinson,
Hashimoto, instead of what
held Daddy in bed groaning
and crying aloud for days
in a darkened room,
hiding from the spears
of any light.

I'm sure that preacher prayed
in his dark gethsemane
*let this cup pass from me,*
and half-skull-pain
is what the Greeks named it.
Me grain, the British say,
as if it were a harvest
of bitter rue and loss,
but more like a final
nail into a cross.

# *Near Florence*

*for Sherry*

My niece and her husband lived
in what they called a double-wide,
but what I call a trailer, plopped down
as if by tornado on red dirt
in the middle of loblolly pines.
Though she'd had a good home
and good schooling, she still chose
to marry him, and live amidst
his many third-place motocross trophies.

And so I thought, well,
that's it then.

But when their baby came
I had to see this child
because she bore the blood
of my only sister who'd died young.
So I flew down to Birmingham
and drove two hours towards
"Alabama's Renaissance City"
just to hold her all Saturday afternoon
on a battered couch, watching *Batman*.

At three I helped him cook "supper,"
watched as he stacked coals, sprayed
lighter fluid, lit them, sprayed more
lighter fluid on the conflagration as I
inched my ass farther up the back steps
so that maybe I wouldn't die in the explosion,
only be maimed, disfigured,
but maybe worth it to incinerate
the idiotic father.

But he brought the "burgers" in safely,
and though I tried to douse the gasoline taste
with ketchup, mustard, onions,
it did no good, and so I ate the raw
and napalmed meat for her, the way
Petrarch kept writing his poems
for Laura even after she was dead,
the way Dante, his love taken
by the slow fire of decay,
fed forever after on the flames.

## *The Gospel of Judas*

I used to think I was blessed—I was young.
Then bad things began to happen. What's wrong?
I asked, sure it was something I'd said or done.
Of course, obvious all along, we die, and alone,

and the process must start somewhere,
in the cataracting eye, the molting hair,
blotch on the skin, in the bone-click of knees.
I wake up patting myself, as if for keys,

checking limbs and organs to see if yet one more
has been washed up on some nightmare, shipwreck shore.
Now for long days at a time I miss
that arrow sense of purposeness,

that walking on bare, stone-toughened feet
to Jerusalem on palm-lined paths to meet
my fate, brief as a passion play,
all pain compressed into a single day.

Instead, too silver-short to retire,
I hobble arthritically past the cock-crow fire
of dithering Peter, brain-tied and tongue-loose,
toward the quick, racking, euthanasia of the noose.

## *The Ghost of Christmas Past*

It's mostly this time of year
that I search for her
in my dreams of coming home
from college for the holidays.

Sometimes we're on our favorite backroad
in the back seat of my '53 Ford,
me doing all the work, since
I was too shy to ask.

In another dream, she was
a bank teller smiling her freckled smile
from her cage across fifty years,
as she told me she was sorry,
that my account was empty,
that I should come back another time.

Funny how long we hold on to happiness,
how long to pain.

Last night I wandered through an old folks home,
thinking I might still recognize her, though
she's an old woman by now, surely
a grandmother, if not
a great one,
though I'm only now a father.

I've looked for her online (who
doesn't?), but I don't know how
to search for something so far gone,
though I've tried everything
I can think of about *love:*
*young, first, great, only, lost.*

## *Tats*

Only carnies had them—hard-bitten,
cigarette-lipped, cadaverous—
and sailors and soldiers, of course.
Back when I got drunk on shore leave
in San Diego, I'd have gotten one too,
if I hadn't passed out.
My lifer buddies could've fixed me good:
an anchor wearing my wife's name,
or a heart swearing *Semper Fi,*
dooming me to a future of bar fights
with Marines who loved to knock off
our Dixie Cups, or with bikers, death skulls
on their skinheads.

And then it was the Age of Aquarius: *Now!*
on the wrist, twining rose on the ankle,
The Great Mandala, *Child*
*of the Universe,* and other such stuff.

Now, what is left? Zen wisdom
from a fortune cookie—Chinese
calligraphy for Kung Pao chicken—
Celtic armbands of wannabe warriors,
symbols of tribes or teams,
the tramp stamps of the doggie position?

And what *will* be left? *This End Up?,*
*Gone But Not Forgotten?,*
the multi-colored county fair
hot-air balloon of ascension,
cocoon of resurrection,
the butterflies on shrink-wrapped skin
now shriveled into Rorschach blots
open to any interpretation.

## *The Late Watch*

With our long, hippie hair stuffed under
cheap wigs, caps on top of those
like billed birds hatching something ugly
on a badly built nest,
we dragged in every weekend.

Draft dodgers, or poor saps like me
who signed on for active duty
and then the reserve to stay out of Nam,
we got up early and drove across the river
to runways on a salt marsh.
I liked early, since the cops were still
sleeping off Friday night, even in
their squad cars, and I could slip my expired
divorce jalopy by.

I trained those dunderheads for four years
how to launch and recover the Ivy League
airline pilots who came to bore holes in the sky,
get combat ready to keep the Viet Cong
off Bourbon Street, though I showed up
for night classes in oil-stained dungarees,
sneered at by both classmates and crew,
and dreamed that when I was free at last
I'd be somebody, maybe find a job
not reeking of jet fuel,
and a new wife who read books.

So, older than any of them, with no other
way out, I sat alone on the pushback tug
by the runway and wrote poems all night
by flashlight for the armadillos
who wandered around me
on the late watch, hoping it would not be
*too* late.

# 4.

# *A World with a Mind of Its Own*

## *Blind Pass*

*"They are all gone into the world of light!*
*And I alone sit ling'ring here..."*
*—Henry Vaughan*

Back about a thousand years ago,
everyone in the family thought
I'd be the first to go, the rake
and ramblin' boy,
now the only one left, Ishmael,
the messenger come to tell Job
his family, too, were all dead:
"I only am escaped to tell thee."

Another morning alive
with no virtues to thank for it,
only vices, and hungover
as usual, I cast into the moon's
silver sunrise pathway on the sea,
then toward its setting in a pink
and violet haze.

My brother long dead
by a head-on drunk,
I ask the universe, Why me?
The sea answers as it always does
with only what it drowns,
never what it saves,
my rod tip nodding,
nodding at the endless waves.

## Deep

We had that in common, both
of our families fighting all the time,
the crockery crashes rocking us to a jumpy sleep
when we stayed over.
The one-week fishing in Florida each year
almost molded us into one flesh.

Later, like two pieces of the same wreckage,
we drifted apart, so that
at the funeral of my preacher father,
it was someone I no longer knew
who washed up, now Matt,
a minister himself, full of advice
and preacherly clichés of consolation.

When they called me with the news
of his death in a head-on, coming back
from a Florida vacation one night,
I could only think of those evenings we spent
standing in the sawdust,
when the fishing boats came in
to unload their catch, and how we walked
on the gray, weathered boards above
the circling fins in the tourists' Deep Sea Pool,
afraid that only one of us
would fall through.

## *Shark Week*

*New Smyrna Beach, Florida*

*Sometimes the shark would go away,*
*sometimes he wouldn't go away. —Quint, Jaws*

*So they cast lots, and the lot fell upon Jonah.*

I wish it were on all day,
every day, like an aquarium,
to remind me of all those summers
up to my neck in the Atlantic,
then the many mornings in the dark,
in the Gulf, up to my heart,
shuffling past the stingrays.

I never *really* worried,
even after I'd felt the tug at my waist
and lifted the stringer to see only the bitten end–
all those speckled sea trout
taken in one gulp.

Now they call the beach,
where my cousin and I rode the waves
for hours, The Shark-Bite Capital
of the World.

Even before I knew what irony meant,
I knew that suburb of Atlanta–
unlike its namesake in antiquity–
could devour me, though I never dreamed
back then how quickly things unseen
could rise from down below
and how you could either listen
to the lifeguard's *Get out, now!*
or hear at the last, *Happy are those*
*who are called to his supper.*

## *St. Simons*

We gathered driftwood, grained
like the ebb and flow of tides,
to shape into living room lamps,
my first wife and I, driving
across the causeway of green
salt marsh and crab-net creeks.
A salt-shaker lighthouse tried
to navigate contrary currents
between islands, reefs, and shoals,
but what did we care, who loved
and would always love, walking
those shark-toothed sands where
waves washed up the wrecks
of ships with all their hopes painted
on broken boards: *Reliant, Endeavor,*
*Faithful, Forever.*

## *Running on Water*

*for Betty*

I dreamed again last night
that you could walk, taking
our hikes in Wales,
fishing from the shore in Florida.
And then you were even wading out,
and suddenly walking over the waves,
like Peter,
only no longer needing
a hand of help. And then,
not just walking, but running
over the blue-green sea
and, far below, making a new reef
for the fish and a harbor
for your ship to come in at last,
your wheelchair.

# *A World with a Mind of Its Own*

*And He said to them, "Cast the net on the right side of the boat, and you will find some." So they cast, and now they were not able to draw it in because of the multitude of fish.*

Ideal conditions, the thunderstorms over, their dark
anvils vaporized into creamsicles, and then the spread,
white sails of Magellanic clouds sailing across
the blue horizon, the surf tranquil once again.

So where are the truant trout, the spooked snook?
Rhetorical question, as if the sea had an answer—
in school, of course.

All the signs are here: merry-go-round dolphins
rising and plunging; squadrons of pelicans,
gangs of gulls, skimming cloud shadows, all
squandered, all seeming to scoff at me.
As if that weren't enough, tubby shell seekers
walk into my line as fine as green sewing thread.

Over the years I've tried it all—fish fortune tellers
watching the weather radar with the robot voice,
*th-hunder sto-horms*—
and pumped the old salts who should be wise
in the ways of the watery underworld.

But everyone has a theory: water too warm or too cold,
tide rising or falling, moon full or dark.
And so I sit. And sit. And sit.
Some wag yells *Try harder!*

I've even prayed for the Bible miracle or to Peter
the Great Fisherman, offered to convert (if I knew what to).
But the sea stays obdurate.

I spend hours looking out, longing for some sign,
some omen, when suddenly one of those cloud shadows
grows and darkens, comes for me, as if jaws already open.
At last, I say aloud. Or at least at *the* last.

Surely some revelation is at hand!

The early sailors thought they were mermaids
riding the waves. But this one, an ugly sea-girl,
lifts her head, eyes me sidewise, snuffs her whiskers,
and goes on down the shore, having seen
nothing important.

## *Blind River*

He (she?) was stretched across the road at 3 a.m.
as we were driving to the boat launch–
must have been ten or twelve feet of him–
lazing on the still-warm asphalt, unimpressed
by horn honking, headlight flashing,
shouting, engine revving.
Finally, he deigned to crawl
on across and let us pass.

As we floated down the river, Alan
shot water moccasins off of the limbs
we passed under, our would-be prey
bass, what Cajuns call "green trout."

Gray algae scummed the surface,
the cypress trees on both sides of us
like columns of a cathedral, its light
stained green by the branches overhead,
Spanish moss often a veil
we had to part.

But all we caught was what they call
a choupique, primeval, snake-headed,
half fish, half eel–creepy,
but said to be good eating–

though I started to throw it back anyway
when asshole Johnny grabbed it
and stuffed a crumpled cigarette package
down its throat,
and they all had a good giggle
as it gagged.

Now, I watch this show about gator hunting,
not because I want to see yet another writhing

death-shot, but to be again, for a while,
among the brackish bayous, salt marshes,
and steamy, cypress-kneed swamps
I loved back then.
And it's consoling to see the gators,
who've lived so long unchanged,
like the descendants of that fish—
its open mouth in memory
as if it might say, could it speak,
*When you've returned to cosmic*
*dust or primeval mud,*
*I will still be here.*

## *Yeti*

I put the expedition together,
and all the boys in the sixth grade
signed up. After all, we needed
doctors, scientists, any kid who'd slogged up
Kennesaw with their father once.
Anyone who had a real tent,
a BB gun, a scout knife.
The girls only scoffed, which was okay,
since they were only girls anyway.

We did our research–*World Book*
from the library on primates, photos
of size 20 footprints splayed
in snow crust, Himalayas, Hillary,
Sherpas, Everest, yaks and maps–
and we were ready to go, face
unafraid that high altitude future,
massive, hairy, strong as we wanted
to grow, a beast as fierce as both
of our parents put together.

## *Aeolus*

The wind never stops, comes straight here
from Nome, not a tree in the way,
just cornfields, though it once
was called Penn's Woods.
It will blow all year, that is
until August, when not a leaf
will stir to cool the sweat.

In Georgia as a boy,
the only wind I saw
blew in the corners of old maps:
the face of Aeolus, curly clouds for hair
puffing his cheeks and huffing
galleons (I thought) to better places,
even into the coils of sea serpents
or whirlpools, then bringing rain
to rinse away the red dirt
and remind me of the sea
somewhere far off, its salt
like poison to the corn.

## *Going Amish*

Their women in the Walmart are hilarious
to this English outlander. Short,
with their ankle-length dresses
and coffee filters over their buns,
they're bespectacled Munchkins.
A few are not bad-looking,
though none in the Kelly McGillis class–
if, that is, you're looking at them lustfully,
hell flames licking at your soles.
Though the wives wear $200 jogging shoes–
to keep up, I guess, with the running of
baking, churning, nursing, canning
on bare wood floors, their blue handwashing
fluttering on the line in the yard–
the men, shod in black brogans,
straw- or black-hatted, jaws beard-fringed,
blue-shirts suspendered, are stooped
and ancient-looking.
You see them as you drive by,
on their mule teams ploughing (not plowing),
dunging, reaping, barn building, baling,
everything green or about to be
all the way to the sky.

When your printer, computer, internet break down
and you're forced to use pen and paper,
the locals say you've "gone Amish."
No microwave, clothes dryer, fridge either.
Only when the storms knock out the power,
and we finally get to tell our stories to those
sitting around us at the kitchen table
and we're slowly joined by the faces
materializing in the candle-lamplight,

do we listen at last as the ghosts get to tell
their stories of a hundred years ago
with nothing to help
but their own voices.

# *Pastorals*

1.

If pride goeth before a fall,
I'm already on my way—
the mid-air man—
like Icarus, wax or wane, I never
could keep them straight.
Floating above the landscape plotted
and pieced, I'll somewhere land,
though trying to steer like those
parachute people, someplace soft
and gentle, like that hay wain, or maybe
even that country churchyard
I see on the horizon,
since what's another elegy
beneath its shaggy, grieving yews and doleful
mooing and tolling bell that seem
to be mourning some tragic event
that has yet to arrive.

2.

Last night, the ploughboys waited
till the sky grew black as the beginning
of *The Wizard of Oz,*
or even the end of the world,
before they turned their teams
toward the barns.
The storm shook the caboose we slept in,
sure that no twister would pick us up
and whirl us away.

In the morning, the land had been rinsed
and the heat quelled, so I drank my coffee

on a wooden deck and watched the long stream
of Amish buggies, their tops down,
their high-stepping horses clip-clopping
on the way to whose home the church was
that week, the fathers long-bearded,
the boys in white shirts buttoned at the wrists
and black vests and hats, their sisters
in sky blue dresses and those coffee-filter buns.

The old steam train rumbled past every hour,
billowing black smoke, so that I felt
I was in another century,
the cornfields and pastures
around and away to the horizon
and the sky now cloudless and blue
except for a wafer of moon
that seemed to bring their God
so much closer than usual.

## *Advent in Ephrata*

*But thou, Bethlehem Ephratah, though thou be little*
*among the thousands of Judah, yet out of thee shall he*
*come forth unto me that is to be ruler in Israel;*
*whose goings forth have been from of old, from everlasting.*
*—Micah 5:2*

We've brought our daughter here
from her birth in Alabama
to grow up near Mommom and Pappy
where it's corn-field flat
and where wooded blue mountains
corral it all.

She's thrilled by black-horsey Amish buggies,
fairy-tale neat farms, barns and fences white
in the morning sunshine, silver silos everywhere,
ploughing mule teams driven by straw-hatted boys
as we drive the backroads to the spire
of Grace Point Nazarene playschool
to learn songs about Jesus, more real
to her now that we pass cows, goats, donkeys,
lambs, more cows, mooing and chewing
in stables full of mangers.

The only blemishes on the centuries-old
bucolic scenes are the juggernauts
of semis, huge-tired tractors, backhoes,
front-loaders, dump trucks everywhere,
even on the narrow roads that right-angle
past the fields, even across stone, one-lane bridges:
Herod Hauling, Judas's Chariots?

Full of what? Milk, the hay baled golden,
more pumpkins, squash, and eggs?

Probably all crops, rolling cornucopia,
as the trees begin their bounty
of beautiful death—
plum, blood-red, lemon, orange—
the flags of farewell,
though the roots reach deep,
and the piglets, lambs, foals,
calves and kids begin to grow
in their mothers.

# 5.

# Everything We Bring, All We Leave Behind

## *As Long As We're Here*

She said it so often, as we wandered
the one-track roads of England,
it became our little joke, always another
duck splash, ducking stool, blue-plaqued
birthplace, deathplace, and all the addresses
in between, until the sun began to set
miles from the nearest pub, Hardy's body
buried one place and his heart (or is it his head?)
interred in another.

And speaking of God, there are churches,
churches everywhere, until
you begin to wonder
if that's all the Normans built,
with lots of bronze lists to look
for your family name or graves
weathered back to the blank stare
of original stone that goes on without us.

But though the lives have been expunged,
not to worry, since all the guidebooks say
the answer we seek (and maybe the pub)
is only five miles farther on
and well worth a look.

# *Everything We Bring, All We Leave Behind*

*The art of losing isn't hard to master.*
*—Elizabeth Bishop*

Supposedly a second chance, but I find
I didn't bring even simple things,
like a single Christmas CD,
though there were plenty of boxes
for all the other Ds:
diseases, debts, doubts, divorce.

Gone missing, a couple of marriages,
a job or two, a few dogs,
fishing in the Gulf, each morning
a layette of blue-green salt water
warm on my belly, sun rising
pearly pink and fuzzy on my back.

Up here,
the only accumulations
piling up at the end
are bitterness
and snow.

The only invitations I get
are to my own pity parties,
and I RSVP to them all.

On an SUV in the parking lot,
the decal of a motorcycle,
the words, "Gone But Not Forgotten,"
and the remains of a name
*yler Li le*

Even my own death is still
packed away somewhere,
attic or cellar, *Your Name Here*
on the packing tape
that's dried up and curled,
ready to let go.

## *Back Then*

when I woke each morning
to a whisper of surf, just a tint
of the coming dawn,
saltwater warm to my waist,
gulls diving, fish biting,
a hot dog for lunch with lemonade
on the porch where I napped
in a hammock while the sun
painted the surf from azure
to aqua, then the lime
of margaritas till time
to boil the shrimp
then troll the shallows
and stroll the beach as the day
prismed into the starry,
palm-fronded dark–
did I know that was heaven back then,
back when I was alive?

## *Spooky Nook Road*

Since I can't afford to fish
the summer surf anymore
and everything here in the corn belt
has wilted, colored khaki as old lettuce
by now, I'm longing for that light
in August that foretells the fall.
And though I also hate holidays,
Halloween seems like a harlequin
heaven at this distance.

Near here is a road where something sad
happened, though none of the Amish
remember what.
No nook anywhere, but the Dutch
is *spuk hus,* maybe a weathered barn
crumbling amid the brown cornstalks,
the scabrous scarecrows only spooky
silhouettes at the full moon, when
the local kids, sick of summer too,
tell stories of headless horsemen
or maybe hear the wind wheeze
through the bones of someone hanging
from a gnarled oak, a seduced
and abandoned suicide,
or some old fisherman swinging
far from the sound of the sea.

## *Sticks*

*Between my finger and my thumb*
*The squat pen rests.*
*I'll dig with it.*
*—"Digging," Seamus Heaney*

Back when I had a hallway, an old umbrella stand
held the walking sticks I brought home, all cut
and carved from the hawthorn hedges
or bramble bushes of Wales,
and like another hedge,
they bristled in the still hallway air
till time for a stroll.

Sharp eyes had seen the future
of the limbs as if already cut
in the mind, trimmed and burnished,
every flaw, the gnarls and furls,
shaken and shaped by Atlantic winds
into weird shapes whose tangles, twined
and twisted, wove fences too thick
for the sheep to breach, too high to leap.
In spring the fringe of every field
bloomed thick and white
like the ermine edges of royal capes.

I know you see the metaphor coming
already, how some hedge-hunter saw growing
what seemed deformed, but a growth that needed
only pruning and the polishing of its flaws
into the root and branch of a sensitive plant
to become like no other, ever,
then or since, like my favorite from
the path to my grandfather's village.

As if he knew I'd own it one day,
it's not some scrawny scribble, but
coppice cut, thick as a shillelagh,
with a topknot, a knurl
like a fist.

## *The 18th Hole*

Even these golden days
of October are forecast
to go south into the north of
the dank and drear of early winter—
an Ohio year:
nine months of anticipation
followed by three months
of disappointment.

The manager complains
that everybody has already
put away their clubs,
but I have always liked
the beginnings of ends,
like mine, alone now,
way over par 72,
putting on the leaf-littered green,
each tree in the slanting light
of late afternoon a struck match
flaring yellow and orange,
ready to light the candles on the cake,
waiting for one last breath.

## *That Night at Barnacle Bill's*

The catfish below our table swarmed to the light
the way they did every night
because assholes like us drank Manhattans
and pitched hush puppies down on their blue-gray
leathery backs, and some wit said
"a regular carp diem," and we even laughed.

How often are you happy?
No, I mean *really* happy,
for a moment, or a meal?

The usual warm salt wind blew in,
and the lights across the bay were a conga line
like stars dropped down on vacation,
and for the whole evening no one
thought about tomorrow, or troubles, or taxes.
Kitsch covered every wall—
life preservers, toilet seats, crab nets, floats;
and the glazed, stuffed fish, though hooked
and long dead and doomed from the first,
seemed to smile down on us;
and when the Brit waitress
asked us over our menus,
"Do you see anything you fancy?"
we howled, because that suddenly seemed
like the funniest question ever,
and we said, "Everything."

## *The Ghosts of Christmas Passed*

It was me they passed
in Walmart this morning, first
my grandfather, stooped, gray, and ball-capped,
his jaw working back and forth as if
chewing a cud or trying to speak.

Then a jingling carol overhead
summoned my sister, her name,
that year dying of a brain tumor, and then
there was my whole family, the dead,
a flock of them, wandering the aisles,
ignoring me, squinting instead
at the shelves as if searching
for something more important.

Then even the living became ghosts too,
and I was surrounded and all alone,
until I looked down at my own hand
now clear as glass.

## *Acknowledgments*

*Barrow Street:* "The Ghosts of Christmas Passed"
*The Cape Rock:* "Forepray"
*Cider Press Review:* "Sticks"
*Connecticut River Review:* "The Ghost of Christmas Past," "Near Florence"
*Crosswinds:* "Elegy in a Time of Peace"
*Ekphrasis:* "Home Is the Sailor, Home from the Sea"
*Evening Street Review:* "Intrusions," "Migraine," "Aeolus"
*Front Range:* "Deep," "Tats"
*Innisfree:* "The Encumbrance of Things Past," "Casualty," "Near Florence," "Hugs"
*Limestone:* "The Unusual Dreams"
*Midwest Poetry Review:* "The Gospel of Judas"
*Pedestal:* "Quarantines"
*Pinyon:* "Snug Harbor"
*Prairie Schooner:* "High Heaven"
*Santa Fe Literary Review:* "Accidents"
*Seems:* "Overtime," "Spooky Nook Road"
*Slant:* "St. Simons"
*Southern Poetry Review:* "Dreaming the Dead," "Murmurs," "As Long As We're Here," "Blind Pass" as ("Requiems"), "All Through the Night," "Yeti"
*Southern Review:* "Advent in Ephrata," "That Night at Barnacle Bill's"
*Spoon River Poetry Review:* "Diminishing Returns"
*Tipton Poetry Review:* "Diminishing Returns," "A Few Thoughts on Death," "Running on Water," "Back Then"
*Verse-Virtual:* "The Welcoming," "Shark Week," "Overtime," "In the Library"

## *About FutureCycle Press*

FutureCycle Press is dedicated to publishing lasting English-language poetry in both print-on-demand and Kindle formats. Founded in 2007 by long-time independent editor/publishers and partners Diane Kistner and Robert S. King, the press was incorporated as a nonprofit in 2012. A number of our editors are distinguished poets and writers in their own right, and we have been actively involved in the small press movement going back to the early seventies.

Each year, we award the FutureCycle Poetry Book Prize and honorarium for the best original full-length volume of poetry we published that year. Introduced in 2013, proceeds from our Good Works projects are donated to charity. Our Selected Poems series highlights contemporary poets with a substantial body of work to their credit; with this series we strive to resurrect work that has had limited distribution and is now out of print.

We are dedicated to giving all of the authors we publish the care their work deserves, offering a catalog of the most diverse and distinguished work possible, and paying forward any earnings to fund more great books. All of our books are kept "alive" and available unless and until an author requests a title be taken out of print.

We've learned a few things about independent publishing over the years. We've also evolved a unique and resilient publishing model that allows us to focus mainly on vetting and preserving for posterity poetry collections of exceptional quality without becoming overwhelmed with bookkeeping and mailing, fundraising activities, or taxing editorial and production "bubbles." To find out more about what we are doing, come see us at futurecycle.org.

## *The FutureCycle Poetry Book Prize*

All original, full-length poetry books published by FutureCycle Press in a given calendar year are considered for the annual FutureCycle Poetry Book Prize. This allows us to consider each submission on its own merits, outside of the context of a traditional contest. Too, the judges see the finished book, which will have benefitted from the beautiful book design and strong editorial gloss we are famous for.

The book ranked the best in judging is announced as the prize-winner in January of the subsequent year. There is no fixed monetary award; instead, the winning poet receives an honorarium of 20% of the total net royalties from all poetry books and chapbooks thes press sold online in the year the winning book was published. The winner is also accorded the honor of being on the panel of judges for the next year's competition; all judges receive copies of the contending books to keep for their personal library.

www.ingramcontent.com/pod-product-compliance
Lightning Source LLC
LaVergne TN
LVHW020049110826
845155LV00029B/694

* 9 7 8 1 9 5 2 5 9 3 3 2 1 *